Dannah Gresh knows that young women want to be in style, look their best and wear the latest. But with that desire comes a huge responsibility. She reminds us in a fun, gentle big-sis type of way that God wants to use our femininity to bring glory to Him. And this involves learning the skill of keeping unique aspects of our femininity for one man, and one man only—our future husband. Through the *Secret Keeper*, Dannah tells it like it is—full of truth and full of power! Definitely a must-read for all young women.

--SUSIE SHELLENBERGER, EDITOR, <u>BRIO</u> MAGAZINE

When teenage guys and adult men find out that I talk to teenage girls in ChikChat, they beg me to beg girls to dress decently. This is a serious issue, where men who really want to follow God, struggle. In *Secret Keeper*, Dannah Gresh gives fresh insight into a guy's mind. Girls who read this book not only learn how a guy thinks and how God thinks, but they are challenged to love and worship God in the area of purity. *Secret Keeper* brilliantly unlocks the mystery of modesty and clearly and cool-ly explains it in a way with which teenagers can identify. *Secret Keeper* also helps the reader feel beautiful and desire to live beautifully and lovingly toward God and others. Every teenage girl has got to read *Secret Keeper*!

--JENI VARNADEAU, INTERNATIONAL RECORDING ARTIST, AND FOUNDER AND HOST OF CHIKCHAT

Secret Keeper

The Delicate Power of Modesty

By Dannah Gresh

MOODY PRESS
CHICAGO

©2002 by
DANNAH GRESH

Book Cover and Interior Design: Julia Ryan [DesignByJulia]
Some Images: www.arttoday.com, Dan Seifert (Stone House Photography)
Image Credit: Hiram Powers, *The Greek Slave*, the collection of the Newark Museum, Gift of Franklin Murphy Jr., 1926: table of contents, pages 9, 14, 59, 67, 72

ISBN: 0-8024-3974-8

1 3 5 7 9 10 8 6 4 2

Printed in the United States of America

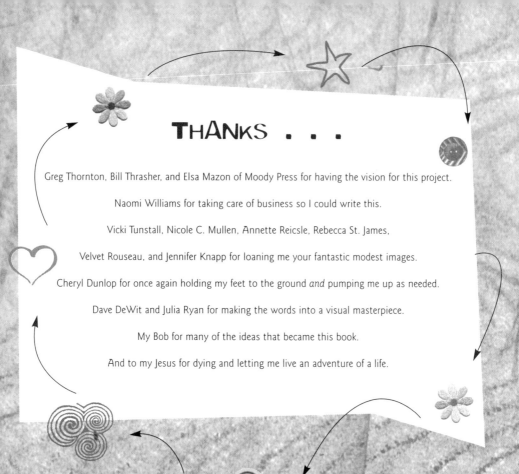

THANKS . . .

Greg Thornton, Bill Thrasher, and Elsa Mazon of Moody Press for having the vision for this project.

Naomi Williams for taking care of business so I could write this.

Vicki Tunstall, Nicole C. Mullen, Annette Reicsle, Rebecca St. James,

Velvet Rouseau, and Jennifer Knapp for loaning me your fantastic modest images.

Cheryl Dunlop for once again holding my feet to the ground *and* pumping me up as needed.

Dave DeWit and Julia Ryan for making the words into a visual masterpiece.

My Bob for many of the ideas that became this book.

And to my Jesus for dying and letting me live an adventure of a life.

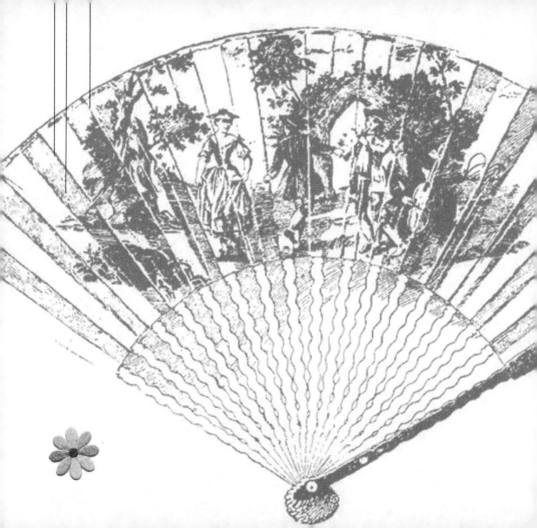

Contents

CHAPTER 1
[The Power]

I sat basking in the warmth of the Florida sunshine when she came my way. Her hot pink jeans were filled with model-thin legs and topped off by a matching tight cotton T-shirt. Her belt and shoes were white leather, pulling everything together in a baby-doll look that pretended to say "innocent" but whispered "sexy."

"Can we talk?" she asked, as a gentle breeze blew her long chestnut mane into her face. She tossed it behind her, revealing deep green eyes.

"Sure, have a seat," I invited.

"I've got a problem," she admitted restlessly. "I, uh . . . well . . . Ya know when you were talking about purity? Well, like, God was telling me something about myself then."

She paused as tears welled up in her eyes, and then she tried once again to verbalize what was causing her pain.

"OK," she said and gave a deep sigh. "I was very overweight until recently. Like, in the last year, I've lost over fifty pounds. And, before that, I didn't really have this problem. I mean, I didn't feel this way. But . . ."

She paused again.

"Well, now, I know that if I wear the right thing, they'll look. I can feel them watching me and . . . well . . ." She hesitated.

"You can feel them watching and what?" I prodded matter-of-factly.

"I like it," she blurted out as another tear began making its way to the rim of her eyelid.

"Then why are you crying?" I asked.

"Because I also hate it," she stated as a free fall of tears streamed down her cheeks. "I hate it because of the way it makes me feel, but I love it because . . . I can't explain it. It's like, well . . ."

I waited for her to find her feelings. I wasn't prepared for her wise discernment.

"It's like I've found this power," she stated confidently and sadly.

If you're reading this book, it's probably because you have the power too. If you're a young woman, you were born with the seed of this power planted firmly within you. Through the years God has tenderly watched that seed grow. Some call it sexuality, but even men possess that. This power is unique to us girls. Some might call it beauty, but that would limit it to the visual. This power is multidimensional.

LOOK

The power is your allure. Allure? Yes, allure. It's a strange, nondescript word. And yet, it *does* give language to the mystifying, undefinable power of the female attraction. A power which both men and women are drawn to, though men with greater magnetism. **I invite you to explore this power with me**. More importantly, we'll explore its source of sustenance. For what good is it to know a power exists if you don't know where to get it? To mention this source is to use a word that's been given a bum rap, but stick with me here.

[The source of the power is modesty.]

Modesty? A source of great power?

Yes. Modesty is the source of this delicate yet formidable power, making it a power in and of itself. It's delicate because it can be so innocently given away without your even knowing it. It's formidable—or difficult to deal with or control—because once you've mastered it, no man will be given access to the full secrets behind your allure until you so desire.

JEN KNAPP stops the show at her concerts with her powerful look. Jen uses layers of dark leather and simple cotton T's for an understated look. She's a striking example that your fashion statement doesn't have to be defined by the trends. She makes her own. So can you!

Do you know Tim Allen, the actor who plays the Tool Time guy on the hit TV sitcom *Home Improvement?* He once wrote that he'd never forget the first time he really noticed a woman's body. "In a way the picture was both frightening and reassuring," he wrote. "I realized for the first time that, dumb as it sounds, all women are naked under their clothes . . . **they have this power and I didn't even know it."**[1]

I'm convinced that the practice of modesty in your life is an intriguing and untapped power source. So I've tackled the challenge of writing this little book. If you stick with me for these few short chapters, you'll be in the driver's seat of this power. I can't say what kind of decisions you'll make with the knowledge, for I won't try to answer *all* the questions, and I promise not to write a list of do's and don'ts for you.

Modesty is much too complex to regulate with a big list of rules. I just want to give you all of the facts in their rawest form so that you can at least make an informed decision about how you'll use this power.

But first, be honest with me. Are you a bit reluctant about reading this? If we're going to lay the facts on the table, we should start with our own feelings.

I'll confess I was not excited to write about modesty. I had a few stubborn misconceptions, and I didn't want my wardrobe rocked. I had to admit that the presence of strong feelings required me to move forward in exploring the topic. With God's help, I decided that this would be the next mountain I would climb. (I felt like I was standing at the bottom of Mount Everest.)

Within just a few weeks of digging into the subject, I found myself frustrated with random thoughts.

"If so many parents of today are troubled by belly rings and tongue rings, how do they explain that Isaac's gift to Rebekah was a nose ring and that during Bible times a pierced nose was a sign of royalty?"

"IT SEEMS TO ME THAT A LOT OF CHRISTIANS AREN'T JUST DISSING THE IMMODEST FASHIONS, BUT FASHION IN GENERAL. SO WHY DOES THE BIBLE ACTUALLY SEEM TO ENCOURAGE US TO DRESS WELL? SCRIPTURE HAS MANY VERSES ENCOURAGING US TO PRESENT OURSELVES BEAUTIFULLY."

IF MODESTY IS SUCH A BIG DEAL, WHY DOESN'T THE BIBLE TALK ABOUT IT MORE? IT'S ONLY DIRECTLY REFERENCED FOUR TIMES.

And my big problem was this: "If immodesty is such a problem, why aren't any of the great Christian leaders of today tackling it with more good ideas and information?"

I was starting from scratch. I felt a little confused and a lot like just throwing in the towel and saying, "I'll wear what I want!" I bet you've got a few stubborn thoughts rolling around in your head too. Here are some I've heard from the teen girls I hang with:

"Why can't I wear what *everyone* else is wearing?"

"Aren't you just hung up on your old sense of fashion? Things change!"

"Why are my parents so hung up on this thing? They just don't get it!"

"Isn't it really the guy's problem? To me it's just fashion!"

Those are good questions. Go ahead and ask the tough questions. I can't promise I'll answer them all, but there is good news. As I've begun this long climb upward, I've changed my mind about how I feel about modesty. I no longer envision some crabby old lady buttoned up to her chin in lace pointing her finger at me. Instead, I see a lovely woman with her long flowing hair tied into a neat bun and her head tilted slightly down. She's holding a robe in front of her, and her hands calmly and perhaps even subconsciously cover her most private parts. Oh, did I mention she is naked? Yes, this beautifully carved 1846 statue entitled *The Greek Slave* by Hiram Powers is now one of the mysterious images of modesty in my mind. Hard to believe? Hey, even the most respected of Protestant ministers in the 1840s favored this statue.

A naked statue? Modest?

My, we do have a lot of ground to cover in this tiny little book, don't we? I hope you'll stick with me. If you don't discover the beauty of this power and the power of this beauty, at least you might discover the hidden modesty in a naked statue.

get this! Modesty is a delicate yet formidable power that God has given to you!

NOTE
1. Tim Allen, *Don't Stand Too Close to a Naked Man* (New York: Hyperion, 1994), 53–54.

As long as you seem to be "hooking up" on a regular basis, no one has a thing to say to you, but if you're alone, people become very concerned and start to give you lots of advice. I listened carefully to all of it when I was alone, but had to conclude—without wanting to seem ungrateful—that the advice young women were getting was just appalling. I was stunned by the way my friends reassured me. You will have many men in your life, they all predicted. Your body's not so bad, your face not so ugly. You'll see, you'll see. You'll do very well on the market. Trust us. Just "maybe put on a shorter skirt or something, stop "hiding" yourself, stop "taking things so seriously." And "you'll see how the men will . . ."

I tuned out at this point, my mind whirring over this You will have many men business. Was that a compliment, I wondered, or a life sentence? It's a life sentence if you're like me, one who hopes for—dare one even say it—not many men but just one. You will have many men. Well, thanks for the generous offer, but am I allowed to decline?[1]

—WENDY SHALIT, A BRILLIANT TWENTY-SOMETHING AUTHOR[1]

I cringe when someone teases my children, Robby and Lexi, about their "girl-friends" or "boyfriends." For crying out loud, they're in elementary school!

It only gets worse when you hit high school, doesn't it? And God forbid you should graduate from college without a boyfriend! At least that's how the pressure often makes it feel.

Is that really what God intended? Was it His plan to have us "try" this guy and then that one like you might a new cosmetic line that advertises, "Try us for 30 days free!" Is it possible that God had something else in mind?

Let's get to the heart of being a woman. God originally created woman to complete . . . fulfill . . . finish man. Check it out. In Genesis 2, God surveys His fine creation and finds everything just right. He uses the word *good*. Everything gets this label . . . with one exception. He says, "It is *not* good for man to be alone."

Hold it one minute there. Did you catch that? *Alone?* The God of the universe was walking and talking with Adam. How could Adam have been *alone?* God could've easily filled that void in Adam. He didn't. Instead, He crafted a masterpiece . . . woman! You are one of those masterpieces. Bill Perkins is an author, but more importantly, he's a man. He writes, "The Master Artist who sculpted the universe spared nothing in the creation of this masterpiece. I've asked men on numerous occasions what they think is the most beautiful sight on earth . . . they'll always say, 'A gorgeous woman.'"[2]

You have been given all of the power of a masterpiece that is worthy of every glance you receive. And ever since Eve, guys have been glancing. Oh, have they been glancing!

Advertising researchers have actually attached little sensors to readers' eyeballs to follow the visual path and figure out what makes someone spend time reading an ad, increasing an advertiser's chance of sales. Crazy, huh? They've discovered lots of little tricks that will increase the viewing time by 1% . . . 2% . . . maybe 3%. But if you really want to stop the reader, use a woman. I've heard different numbers, but it seems a photo of a woman will increase the length of time someone spends with an ad by 14 to 30%. That's way more than anything else. It didn't matter much whether it was a woman or a man doing the looking. Both were drawn to the beauty of the female image. (There's that allure!) Advertisers just don't get the same response when they use the image of a man, no matter how fantastic looking he might be. It's the masterpiece called "woman" that calls our eyes to praise. The masterpiece is applauded with many glances. Just how powerful is the draw? Let's get a guy's perspective on this. Author Henry Rogers writes about how incredibly beautiful women are. He says that if it is the bottom of the ninth in the seventh game of the World Series . . .

(. . . OK, a big moment for guys . . .)

and the home team is down by three runs and has two outs with the bases loaded . . .

(. . . the stakes are getting higher . . .)

and the home-run king is at the plate . . .

(. . . now this is a major life moment for guys . . .)

and suddenly a beautiful woman pulls off her top . . .

. . . the guys would forget the game!

(Now THAT'S power!)

He writes, "Women are beautiful to us because God made them that way. Their beauty and our desire are God-given. The nakedness of a woman has a powerful impact on us."[3]

Our bodies create quite a stir in guys. Let's be specific here. *Your* body can really drive a guy crazy. And that's what God intended. Check out Proverbs 5:18–19 where it tells a man to "rejoice in the wife of your youth. . . . May you ever be captivated by her love." That word *captivated* would be better translated "intoxicated" since that's what the Hebrew writer was trying to suggest. Imagine this . . . your husband on your wedding night filled with a holy drunken stupor at your presence. That's what God wants for you one day *if* His plan for you includes marriage.

But there's a catch. Notice the earlier part of the passage where it says, "*the* wife". . . in other words, *one* woman. Again and again, the Bible reconfirms that this intoxication is only to be shared with one guy . . . and after you're married.

Until then, it's under wraps . . . a secret to be shared with your husband. Sure, you could "have many men," but God says "just one." Until then, the fullest secrets of the incredible masterpiece of your body are to be your unique secret.

As you might have noticed, some girls today aren't the best secret keepers. They flaunt their bodies in hip huggers complemented by belly rings, miniskirts matched to high heels, tight shirts to go with tighter pants and . . . well, I could go on, but you've probably had some of that stuffed down your throat already.

Am I saying we have to hide all of your beauty and cover ourselves head to toe? No, I'm not saying that. If your experience is like mine, you've had some well-intentioned Christians tell you to dress pretty unattractively. (At least, that's what I perceived they were telling me.) The Bible doesn't tell us to walk around with a sack on our head and with the God-given curves of our body flattened by a corset before they're covered in a black sack.

may you ever be captivated by her love.

Let's get one thing clear; fashion is OK. And, though **God implores us to be more concerned with our inner beauty than our external beauty,**[4] He provides a consistent theme in the Bible for *appreciating* external beauty. (Why do you think He made us "masterpieces" so devastatingly beautiful?) Sarah was so beautiful that ol' Abraham was afraid other men might kill him so they could have his wife. Rebekah was "very beautiful" and a "virgin." Abigail was "intelligent and beautiful." Esther is perhaps the Bible character most acclaimed for her beauty. There are more. The fact that their beauty is even mentioned in a document that doesn't waste words is significant. These were precious words. It must have been important to note the beauty of these women.[5]

Did these beauties of the Bible appear plain and without use of the fashion of the day? Not necessarily. Several times the Bible notes that beautiful women used cosmetics to make themselves more beautiful.[5] Esther was even pampered for twelve months!

And fashion? You got it, babe! If you lived in those days you might have a "wimple." If you really wanted to look great, you'd get a "stomacher."[6] (Wimple? Stomacher? I don't think I want to know more! What crazy names.) A wealthy girl might receive a nose ring for a kind of engagement ring. Isaac gave one of these to Rachel. Fashion then was as strange as fashion today. (Stick with me, though, because there were some very important differences in the expression of style. That culture knew the power of modesty.)

Beauty and fashion aren't condemned by the Christian faith. On the contrary, beauty seems to be nearly synonymous with God's glory. In the book of Revelation, God is described in undeniable splendor. Things we consider to be beautiful seemed to adorn Him in John's vision of heaven. Revelation 4:3 says that God sat on His throne, and He was so amazingly beautiful that the writer said He "had the appearance of jasper . . . a rainbow, resembling an emerald, encircled the throne." Moses actually saw God's beauty, in part. God's glory was so powerful that Moses had to settle for seeing the back of God. It was so powerful that after he received the Law from God, Moses' face literally glowed. Beauty is one of God's greatest expressions. I think it's only fitting that we, created in His image, strive to express ourselves through beauty as well. So, express it!

You were created as a masterpiece and *you* are one of God's expressions of beauty. Short, tall, thin, thick, freckles, big eyes, small ones . . . it doesn't matter.
[Your beauty is powerful].

Don't believe me? Do you think you are too tall? Too short? Too heavy? Yeah, I know how that feels. Sadly, most of us really struggle with those feelings. In fact, I've heard that most women or girls who spend time looking at a fashion magazine actually end up feeling depressed about their own bodies. Who wouldn't? Little of what you see in those magazines is real. The girls are all "lighted," "make-uped," "touched-up," and "computer-generated" to "perfection" . . . a standard that's unattainable for you or me or even the model in the picture!

I spent most of my teen years doing my hair and makeup in the dark because I so despised how I looked. I can identify with not "feeling" beautiful. Isn't it interesting how Satan has taken this unique gift and power of ours and made us believe we are actually ugly! He is such a big fat liar! He's established standards that are hollow lies, and when we don't look "lighted," "make-uped," "touched-up," and "computer-generated," then we feel ugly, even though the standard is not even a reality.

What does God say? He says He looks down upon you and is "*enthralled* by your beauty"! (Psalm 45:11, italics added). Wow! Think of that. The God of the universe, looking down at your uniquely chiseled features, coloring, and size, is *enthralled* by your beauty. Not just Miss America's. Not just today's hottest stars . . . yours! You're uniquely beautiful. Express it. Just be sure to keep the most powerful part of your beauty as a secret for one man.

I want you to know God's purpose for you. Of course, that's a big subject, but part of your specific purpose is related to your beauty. You were created to express God's beauty, and, if His plan is for you to marry one day, part of your purpose is to "intoxicate" one man with that beauty.

Oh, you are beautiful enough to have many men, but God's plan is for you to share the power of your beauty with *one man*. Will you have many men? Or will you dare to romantically dream of just one?

Well, buckle up, friend. All this beauty stuff is the warm and fuzzy part of this book. Ready to get to the heart of this modesty issue? We're going to go deep with one of the Bible's key words. I'll warn you now. We're going to unlock a powerful truth from the Bible. It's not for the faint of heart.

get this!

God's intended purpose for you as a carefully crafted masterpiece is to "intoxicate" <u>one man</u> with the fullest extent of your beauty.

NOTES
1. Wendy Shalit, *A Return to Modesty: Discovering the Lost Virtue* (New York: Simon & Schuster, 1999), 36.
2. Bill Perkins, *When Good Men Are Tempted* (Grand Rapids: Zondervan, 1997), 13.
3. Henry J. Rogers, *The Silent War* (Green Forest, Ark.: New Leaf Press, 1999), 68.
4. 1 Peter 3:3–4.
5. Sarah, Genesis 12:11; Rebekah, Genesis 24:16; Abigail, 1 Samuel 25:3; Esther 2:7, 9.
6. Easton's Bible Dictionary, posted on www.crosswalk.com, accessed on 9/25/01.
7. Perkins, *When Good Men Are Tempted*, 10.

CHAPTER 3
[The Mark!]

It was the night that Lisa Ryan, now a cohost on the 700 Club, would be passing on her Miss California crown. She'd spent the year professing Christ and building up what the producers of the show called a "good girl" image. A special gown was designed just for her final walk down the runway, but the producers didn't think it was sexy enough. They called for it to have the cleavage cut to the waist and for the slit of the skirt to run to the top of her thigh.

"I was uncomfortable with the suggestions," writes Lisa in her book For Such a Time as This. "But I was a people pleaser. I didn't value myself enough or have the confidence to say no so the designer made the changes. To be honest, I was a little intrigued by the attention and sense of power it gave me. I still remember that final walk. The dress was a showstopper, all right, but I had crossed the line, and I knew it. I was a Christian and that dress didn't portray the elegance and integrity that I wanted to be remembered for."[1]

ITS JUST FASHION. That's what a lot of girls think.

Is it *just* fashion?

I'd like to push you . . . stretch you . . . challenge you. I'll do it all with just one word. Are you ready? Once I discovered this Hebrew word in the Bible, it revolutionized my thinking about how I present myself. Will you stick with me through this? Here we go!

I'd like to talk to you about sin. How would you define sin? Take a moment and write your thoughts here:

Let's see how your thinking lines up with the truest meaning of sin in the original Hebrew and Greek version of God's Word. The constructions of the original Hebrew and Greek languages are so different from modern language. The deep, beautiful truths of God are often weakened in our translations. I think that has happened with the concept of sin.

The Hebrew culture revolved around war, so many of the Hebrew words are archery terms. The main Old Testament Hebrew root word for sin is *Chatta* (or *hatta*). To pronounce that you kind of spit out a hard "h" sound and add "atta"! Try it.

[Ch-atta!]

Its meaning most literally translates "to miss the mark." Picture an archer's target. What do you most desire to hit? **The *bull's - eye!*** That's the "mark." The intended purpose of aiming your arrow is to hit that prized center mark. Spiritually, the bull's-eye is God's intended purpose for you. He delights in your hitting the mark because He knows that, since this is what you were created for, it will be most fulfilling. Of course, it's a bit more complicated than that, but just this basic definition was a revolutionary view of sin for me.

God isn't up there saying, "Bad! Bad girl! You really messed up!" He is up there saying, "Oh, My sweet masterpiece, do you have any idea the fantastic blessing you just missed? I can't reward you with the prize now, but try again. Come on;

with My help you can do it. Hit the mark!" Isn't that amazing? How God loves us. His standards are demanding. The bull's-eye *is* small, but His own definition of sin is packed with far more grace than our handed-down definitions and perceptions.

Let's look at this word, *Chatta,* a little more closely. It's easy to measure sin when we see someone miss the target altogether. Adultery is a good example. Can you think of some other sins where the entire target is missed? Add a few to our target below, placing these "big nasties" off of the target.

Now, you and I both know that sin doesn't have to be this "big" to still be sin. Look at all that space on the target between actually missing it and skillfully hitting the bull's-eye. The meaning of *Chatta* doesn't say we "missed the target." It says we **"missed the mark"**—the dead center of the target . . . the bull's-eye. That's the mark! You can actually hit the target without hitting the bull's-eye, can't you?

We often don't even perceive these sins in our life. Sometimes we just get caught up in the motion of everything around us, and instead of trying to mirror God's holiness, we just mirror the world around us. Without willfully defying God, we sin. Can you think of some ways that we sometimes miss the bull's-eye but not the target altogether? Gossip sure is a great example of this kind of sin, isn't it? I hate gossip, and yet sometimes I'm confronted with the fact that by hanging around it, I've condoned it. Worse yet, I sometimes stick in a few jabs myself, masking them with concern and "prayer requests."

Add a few of your own to the target,

placing them on the target but not in the bull's-eye.

GOSSIP

God's Best

Now I don't want you to think that God has "levels" of sin. He doesn't. It all separates us from Him. It's all sin. I'm just trying to show you how very specific God's Word is. You can think you are "pretty close" to God's intended purpose for you and still miss the mark. It's still sin. God's target would probably look like this.

I'm wondering, Did you include immodesty on any of your other targets? I placed it here on this one so it would stick out. (You knew *that* was coming, didn't you?) Can you be living a really clean life as far as not even dating guys or having anything physical to do with them and still sin in the area of your sexuality? I think you can.

Remember, the bull's-eye represents God's intended purpose for your life. In the area of sexuality His purpose is for you is to be an expression of His beauty and to "intoxicate" *one* man with that beauty. *One man!* That's the key.

Let me explain to you a little bit of what happens when a guy is "intoxicated." Many of our bodies' responses are activated by the autonomic nervous system (ANS). This system is not controlled by the will, but by the environment. For example, do you remember getting lost when you were young? Chances are your parents weren't far away, but do you remember that sick feeling in your stomach and the rapid pulse? Perhaps, like me, a hot flash hit you. You felt physically different because of the fear that the environmental change—no mom or dad—presented.

You cannot control these reactions by choice. **That's how the ANS works**. It forces the body to respond to the environment.

Sexual arousal works the same way. Things in the environment—what we see, what we hear, and what we smell—work together to tell the brain that the time is right for sexual response. The brain sends chemicals through the body. This is particularly strong in a guy since he is created to be visually stimulated. If he sees a young woman walk by him wearing revealing clothing, his ANS can be activated. What happens in his body? He may notice the change in his pulse, his body temperature will rise, and blood begins to pump rapidly through his body. The arousal process has begun. For a guy this is very strong and presents clear physical changes. It can be hard for us girls to understand just how powerful it is since sexual attraction offers far less of a physical change in us and is harder to define. It's sometimes overwhelming for guys to walk through a mall past larger-than-life posters in Victoria's Secret and The Limited or to pass by a magazine rack covered with pictures of half-naked women. Although he can choose how to respond to this arousal, he cannot control that it has occurred. **It's the environment that controls it.**

How hard is it for a guy to make righteous choices once the ANS has been activated? Very difficult. The Bible says that when sin is conceived, it gives birth. In other words, once that desire is there, it's aching to be released. Altering the course of the full birth of lust once aroused is very difficult for a guy. I'm not saying a guy has no responsibility to control his own arousal. He is completely responsible for his sexual advances. But sometimes a girl can attract the wrong kind of guy with what she wears. I don't even mean a really, really bad guy. You could just attract a really, really nice guy whose moral standards have been suddenly and terribly weakened. The next thing you know, you're in a relationship that's headed down the wrong path fast.

Think I'm exaggerating? Ask your dad his opinion!

How **short** is too short?

"WE TALK ABOUT MODESTY BEFORE OUR BRIO MISSION TRIPS IN LETTERS WE MAIL OUT. WE ARE GIVING THEM PERMISSION TO WEAR SHORTS, SLACKS, AND JEANS. OUR RULE OF THUMB IS 'SIT DOWN IN FRONT OF A FULL-LENGTH MIRROR SITTING INDIAN STYLE WEARING YOUR SHORTS, AND IF YOU CAN SEE UP YOUR LEGS, THAT'S TOO SHORT FOR YOU. IF A GIRL IS SITTING INDIAN STYLE OR SHE'LL EVEN JUST CROSS HER LEGS AND SIT IN FRONT OF A MIRROR, SHE'LL SEE WHAT EVERYONE ELSE SEES.'"

--SUSIE SHELLENBERGER, EDITOR, BRIO MAGAZINE

This temptation is real in even the strongest of Christian guys. Susie Shellenberger, editor of Focus on the Family's *Brio* magazine, was hangin' with Superchic[k], a great Christian guy's band. The leader of the group, Max, really laid it on the line as far as what skimpy dressing does to the band members. He told how they'd be playing a Christian festival and when they'd scan the audience they'd see girls sitting Indian style in very short shorts or skirts. They'd see girls in things that were way too low or tight. The temptation this created was so strong that as soon as they finished their set, they'd leave the stage and dive into the Bible or pray so that they'd not be caught up in lustful thoughts. What a righteous response. They were choosing to override their ANS through God's power. But isn't it sad that they had to go to such extremes when they'd rather be mixin' with the audience after a set? These are *Christian* guys ministering at a *Christian* event

... do not cause anyone to stumble.

... do not cause anyone to stumble.

tempted by *Christian* girls who have no clue about how they are causing their Christian brothers to stumble.

What does the Bible say about that? It is emphatic . . . very clear! First Corinthians 10:32 says "Do not cause anyone to stumble." What an uncomfortable challenge for those of us who've been fooled into thinking *it's just fashion!*

Ephesians 5:3 pushes us just a bit more out of our comfort zone. It says, "But among you there must not be even a hint of sexual immorality, or of any kind of impurity, or of greed, because these are improper for God's holy people." Get that? Not a *hint* of sexual sin. Have we hinted at sexual sin when we wear the tight T-shirt, the low-cut blouse, the short skirt?

God's purpose for you sexually is to "intoxicate" *one man*

WE try hard to make our dance moves athletic and skillful, not sensual. We want to exude energy and joy-without looking like Britney Spears. We want to keep it cute and clean, so we don't show our bellies and we don't wear anything too tight." It's fun to overhear some of the girls telling others, "You can't wear that." or "We can't do that move." They know where I stand, and I hope they're learning how to draw a few lines of their own.

--NICOLE C. MULLEN, SINGER/SONGWRITER
(Talking about she and her "adopted" younger sisters dress and dance preferences. She originally connected with some of these girls when she was teaching dance at a Y.M.C.A. She takes a few of the girls in the class with her when she tours.)[2]

with your beauty. That's the bull's-eye. When you dress immodestly, you create arousal in *many* men. That is missing the mark. Is it just fashion? No. Immodesty is *sin.*

[**Rough truth, huh?**] But truth it is. Narrow-minded? The path *is* narrow to pleasing God, but, oh, the rewards are so incredibly unfathomable.

When we hit the mark, God blesses us. In fact, when you get to the Greek New Testament, the word for sin is *hamartia,* which means "to miss the mark and *so not share in the prize.*" Here, the word for sin actually speaks of the reward, the blessing, the benefit of living according to God's specific purpose for our lives. He loves to bless you and me!

God's bull's-eye for your sexuality is that it be a free and fulfilling expression of your love for one man. He's clear about that one man thing. Some of today's most credible studies of sexuality affirm that those who wait to have sex until they are married tend to be more sexually satisfied. *USA Today* once ran an article detailing how the Christian view of waiting for sex until marriage seemed to actually create a more fulfilling sex life. They entitled the article, "The Revenge of the Church Ladies"! Receiving God's gift of sexuality, God's way, results in rewards.

Imagine how fulfilling it will be if you save it all . . . every moment of passion . . . every bared curve . . . every suggestive glance! Imagine the powerful "intoxication" you'll create for the man of your dreams if you keep the deepest secrets of your beauty just for him.

Of course, knowing there's a payoff doesn't simplify the debate. Just where do you draw the line between fashion and hitting the mark? Let me take you a bit further into the minds of men.

> "I'll never have any suitors."
> --THE BEAUTIFUL MEG IN THE MOVIE LITTLE WOMEN

> "You don't need scores of suitors. Only one, if he is the right one."
> --LITTLE AMY SETTING HER STRAIGHT

get this! Since immodesty creates arousal in many men, it misses the mark of God's intended purpose for you. It's not just fashion. It's sin.

NOTE

1. Lisa Ryan, *For Such a Time as This* (Sisters, Ore.: Multnomah, 2001), 26.
2. Today's Christian Woman, March/April 2002, Article by Camerin Courtney, pg. 86.

Do you have a "most embarrassing moment"?

I sure do.

Once I stood up on the driver's side of my minivan, the door wide open, while I bent over the seat to reach my stuff. It was a loooong reach. As I turned to slam the door shut with my arms loaded, I noticed a guy sitting in his car right beside me with his jaw dropped so low that his mouth looked like the Grand Canyon. His face was red when I caught him staring.

That's when the draft hit me. A cool spring breeze announced to me that the hem of my skirt was wrapped up around my waist and my panties were the featured view. You can guess who was blushing then!

I was on the way to my high-paying, high-profile, fast-paced advertising agency when that happened several years ago. OK, so it wasn't high-paying or high-profile, just fast-paced, but it was intriguing. I learned some of the amazing tricks that advertisers use to control our pocketbooks . . . and our minds. Most interesting to me is how they use women's bodies. Let me share with you two important advertising secrets that will either forfeit or claim the power of your body.

Lesson Number One:

[Showing Less Controls More]

Let me tell you about the Gestalt theory. (Warning: College-level brain food ahead!) The Gestalt theory teaches a graphic designer to control a viewer's time by forcing the person to mentally complete a visual image. Because the brain is intrigued by completing the incomplete, it will always pause to finish an unfinished picture. **Check out this trio of circles. What else do you see?**

You think you see a triangle, because that's the most common image that your brain wants to use to complete this.

 **Check out this next little graphic. Describe what you see.**

People say they see a person, even though this is just a few squiggly lines. Why? We naturally seek to continue visual elements. This is the Gestalt principle of continuity.

What does a guy see when a girl walks by him wearing a long, tight skirt with a slit all the way up the sides? He sees past the fabric, because the slit invites him to finish the picture. This is simple visual science.

How do you think this theory works when a girl wearing a tight T-shirt shirt with her belly bared walks down the street past a guy? Yikes! Because he sees an incomplete picture of her body, he is compelled to complete it. The thrill *not* of what is seen, but what is yet to be seen is what actually tempts him. His imagination kicks in. It's just how the brain works, especially for guys.

It's much more tempting for a guy to see a girl dressed in today's skimpy fashion than it would be to see her naked. Does that astound you? It's true. A Christian couple I know recently went to France for vacation. At one point this pair unwittingly stayed in a hotel next to a nude beach. The woman was concerned it would be tempting for her husband. It wasn't. In fact, he was rather grossed out. There was nothing left to the imagination, which is the most tempting part of immodesty. The control comes from the unfinished picture and the imagination that it takes to complete it. If a guy sees a girl walking around in tight clothes or a miniskirt or tiny shorts . . . well, she might as well hang a noose around the neck of his spiritual life. It's not "just" fashion but a constant source of spiritual failure for men.

Showing just a little bit of your belly . . . a touch of your bra strap under a tight spaghetti string T-shirt . . . the curve of your hips under a tight skirt . . . well, you get the idea. Showing a little can be devastating to a guy who wants to please Christ.

I have a confession to make. That day that my skirt tried to strangle me, I'd *created* my own most embarrassing moment. My skirt was too short and too tight, but I really thought it was "just" fashion that made me look good. Though I did not struggle with immodesty before I was married, I did find myself falling prey to fashion's sexually suggestive whims after I was out from under my parents' watchful eyes. (Once my dad sent me back to my room to change because my *shoes* were too immodest. My *shoes*, for cryin' out loud! I really had an attitude that morning.) But when I started making the calls on my own as a young married woman, I sometimes didn't choose well, and for that I'm sorry. Are you ever guilty of the same kinds of choices? Or do you find yourself grumbling when your parents "force" modesty standards on you?

I KNOW how hard this is. Sometimes I walk through a mall or along a crowded sidewalk, and I see heads turning toward a girl who's dressed like the girls on the Limited posters, complete with tight jeans, a tight T-shirt, and her belly bared. And . . . are you ready for this true confession . . . *I wish it were me turning heads!* Don't you feel that way sometimes? We ache to be noticed and adored. That's where knowing these advertising tricks could get dangerous. I know that you could abuse the power of your allure even more now that I'm sharing these secrets with you. Please don't do that. I think you'll miss the deeper truth behind the power of your body, which brings me to another great trick of advertisers.

Lesson Number Two:

[Perceived Value Increases Worth]

In my early days in the marketing business, we designed company logos for about $1,250. One day, because we were concerned with how time-consuming the logos were, we hiked our prices up . . . to $8,000. We expected to have far less logo work to do, but instead, we had more! It was the perceived higher value that drove the demand . . . and the worth of the project. When clients perceived that this project required not only a great deal of financial investment but also a patient investment of time, they wanted it *badly*.

The same principle is at work when you dress. Immodesty removes the obstacles and invites any passing guy to desire you in his mind. It's a cheap thrill requiring no investment on his part. It offers him the power of your body at *his* control. He is motivated by lust.

Modesty protects the true secrets of your body for one man, requiring him to invest into your life in order to one day enjoy your allure. It invites a guy to earn your virtue. Finding love this way is a long and slow process, and it often seems

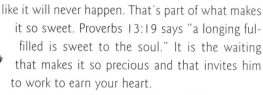

like it will never happen. That's part of what makes it so sweet. Proverbs 13:19 says "a longing fulfilled is sweet to the soul." It is the waiting that makes it so precious and that invites him to work to earn your heart.

He is motivated by love.

How does he do this? Through romance! I don't know about you, but I'll take the candlelight dinners, soft love songs, and carefully crafted love notes of yesterday over today's "liberated" casual sex scene. Wendy Shalit challenges, "Did men court women in the past because they found it more fun than casual sex? No, it was because women's modesty required it!"[1]

Some men perplex me. They can chase after all the "hot" girls and even have sex with them, and yet when it comes to true love they consistently state that they want the modest, pure girl. An MTV special on guys and sex once featured two guys whose goal was to have a different girl every night. And they often did. But they made it clear that when they were serious about a relationship, they'd never go for "that kind" of girl.

who Can a Girl Count on for **Good** Advice?

"ONE OF THE TEEN GIRLS THAT COMES ON OUR MISSIONS TRIPS HAS A BROTHER WHO IS A REALLY STRONG CHRISTIAN. A LOT OF TIME, SHE SAYS, 'HE WILL COME TO ME AND SAY "RACHEL, YOU SHOULDN'T BE WEARING THAT!"' RACHEL WILL SAY, 'I DON'T SEE ANYTHING WRONG WITH THIS!' AND HER BROTHER, RYAN, WILL SAY, 'YEAH, BUT FROM A GUY'S POINT OF VIEW HERE'S WHAT'S GONNA HAPPEN IN OUR MINDS.' IT'S SMART TO ASK AN OLDER BROTHER HIS OPINION OF YOUR CLOTHES IF HE'S A GOOD CHRISTIAN GUY. OR YOU CAN ASK YOUR DAD. THEY'RE GOING TO BE QUICK TO TELL YOU WHAT'S HAPPENING IN A GUY'S MIND."

--SUSIE SHELLENBERGER, EDITOR, BRIO MAGAZINE

When your perceived value is high because you've protected your reputation and your sexuality, there are obstacles between you and all men. These obstacles issue a challenge for men to earn your heart. Flowers, Valentine's Day gifts, and romantic dinners are some of the ways a man might try to prove himself worthy of your virtue.

No matter how much temporary attention immodesty may gain you, it will never equal the thrill of passion that follows a life protected by the power of modesty. Does it mean you'll be less attractive? No, it means quite the opposite. (I'll never figure a guy's mind out.) Here's what my husband has to say about it:

Dannah presented herself with impeccable modesty. It didn't dampen my desire for her. In fact, I think it fueled it. The fact is, she could've worn a burlap sack and I'd have been attracted to her. I can't explain it, but a guy yearns most for what he can't have. Because Dannah did not freely give herself, I desired to earn her.

--BOB GRESH

OK, I don't know about "impeccable" modesty, but my parents were closely watching what I wore. Today, I'm glad they did. I realize it was a key factor in requiring Bob to romance me.

Admit it. You want to be desired! The question is, Will you be desired by guys looking for a cheap thrill in their minds, or will you be romantically and passionately pursued because your modesty demands it?

[Modesty is the first line of defense for your purity.]

When a guy with true interest in you perceives that this has been protected, he will rise to romance you and earn your heart. It may not happen for a few years, and it certainly may seem as if you've been overlooked—oh, the waiting is so hard—but the best things in life are worth the wait.

No question about it—the advertising world uses the female body to control spending. But now, you know two of the most powerful secrets of advertising. What will you do with them?

FASHION CHALLENGE:
FASHION CHALLENGE:
FASHION CHALLENGE:

[What Are You Advertising?]

So, what's a girl to do with all the "just" fashion mentality that advertisers throw her way? I'd recommend you start in your closet. Why not take inventory of your wardrobe today? Do this with a friend. It's much more fun and it's important. It's as easy as 1, 2, 3.

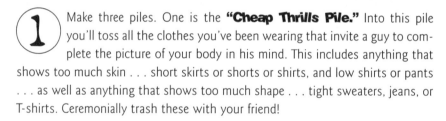

1 Make three piles. One is the **"Cheap Thrills Pile."** Into this pile you'll toss all the clothes you've been wearing that invite a guy to complete the picture of your body in his mind. This includes anything that shows too much skin . . . short skirts or shorts or shirts, and low shirts or pants . . . as well as anything that shows too much shape . . . tight sweaters, jeans, or T-shirts. Ceremonially trash these with your friend!

2 The second pile is your **"Power Pile,"** into which you'll throw anything that actually hides the secrets of your alluring body in a fashionable and comfortable manner. These go back in your closet and drawers. These items make up a part of your very high price tag that will require one man to pay a very high price to earn your heart.

③ The final pile? That's your **"Fuzzy Friend Pile."** You're a bit "fuzzy" on these items. They could go either way, so you're going to ask your friend to make the decision for you. Whatever she says goes. Don't compromise.

get this! The allure of immodesty is not in what is seen but what is not seen. Modesty issues a challenge for one man to romantically earn your virtue.

NOTE
1. Wendy Shalit, *A Return to Modesty: Discovering the Lost Virtue* (New York: Simon & Schuster, 1999), 146.

CHAPTER 5
[The Inner Quality]

1000 B.C. * BATHSHEBA * ON A ROOFTOP

Up on the rooftop, she tilted the clay pot, splashing her bare arms and hands. Laying the pot to her side, she loosened the tight belt around her waist, allowing her light cotton robe to blow in the breeze. She stood there with her head tilted and her eyes closed, enjoying the sensual feeling it gave her to stand in a loose garment. Had she been seen in the streets like this she'd have been punished, as a man or woman without his or her belt was considered nude.

She could've bathed like this. She often did, but it was just too tempting to let herself enjoy just a bit more freedom. Turning her front toward the wall, she slipped the robe off of her shoulders, allowing it to dangle around her waist, accentuating the fullness of her hips and the curving frailty of her waist. She lifted the pot and poured the cool water, enjoying the rush of it as it wetted her bare back. She brought the pot to her chin and released the remaining liquid across her breasts, carefully bared to only the clay wall in front of her. She stroked herself gently, enjoying the refreshing cleansing of her bare skin.

She was beautiful.

She stood there drying in the breeze enjoying the freedom.

Someone might be watching.

A.D. 2001 * BRITNEY * ON A STAGE

The hydraulic lift began to hoist her into the thunderstorm. Her translucent cowboy hat quickly filled with water. She walked further into it, tossing her head as the cascade wetted her body. Her tight jeans, now wet, were low enough to reveal softly curved round hips and a gentle feminine belly. She turned, touching herself sensually as the light caught the sequins in her seemingly backless bra.

In a low breathy voice she began to sing as the water dripped down her soft skin.

She stood there glistening in the light. She stroked herself gently, enjoying the refreshing wetness on her bare skin.

She was beautiful.

She stood there in the light enjoying the freedom.

People were watching.

We often hear of King David's sin. Adultery. It was a "biggie." He missed the target altogether. But he was not alone. Why don't we talk about Bathsheba's sin?

We don't know that she bathed nude. In fact, it's often suggested that she didn't. Many fifteenth-century expressions of art show Bathsheba dressed. It was not the clothes she wore or did not wear that were immodest. It wasn't because she was being careful to hide the secret power of her allure that David's body was aroused. It *could* have been that Bathsheba, in a state of loneliness caused by a husband gone to battle, desired spectators.

Thousands of years later, women still commit this sin of thoughtless and careless exposure. Britney Spears's 2001 Thanksgiving special featured her wet and exposed, though not nude. Is she ignorant to the fact that she is prostituting herself visually? Maybe. Her greater sin is not in what she wears, but that she desires spectators to lust after her.

[**My point is this, friend.**] We must look past the clothes. Fashion trends change from culture to culture. In Madagascar, a woman's exposed arms are considered very sexual. Doesn't that sound ridiculous?

I've mentioned that Isaac sent a nose ring to Rebekah as a sort of engagement ring. It said more

Rebekah:
A Woman of Fashion and Discretion

REBEKAH ACCEPTED ISAAC'S NOSE RING. YOU WILL FIND LOTS OF TODAY'S TEENS DONNING THE SAME "FASHION." BUT WATCH REBEKAH AFTER SHE RECEIVES THAT NOSE RING. SHE'S TAKEN TOWARD ISAAC IN A FIELD, AND AS SHE SEES HIM COMING TOWARD HER, SHE COVERS HER FACE WITH A VEIL. THIS DISPLAY OF MODESTY . . . SAVING THE SECRETS OF HER BEAUTY . . . COMES JUST HOURS BEFORE SHE IS ALONE WITH HIM IN A TENT TO CONSUMMATE THEIR MARRIAGE. REBEKAH KNEW HOW TO WEAR THE FASHION OF THE DAY AND HOW TO PROTECT HER VIRTUE. THE CHALLENGE FOR US TODAY IS TO KNOW WHEN WE CAN WEAR THE FASHION AND WHEN WE SHOULD COVER UP!

than "marry me." It also said, "I'm rich." A nose ring was reserved for the upper class and was a sign of royalty. You won't find Laura Bush wearing a nose ring, because they don't have the same appeal among the upper crust in our culture today.

Today in Western culture, the bare belly button is a raving statement of sensuality (as if you hadn't noticed). I mean, think about it! It's a belly button! It even sounds funny . . . belly button. But our culture has trained us to find it sexy . . . at least for now.

Culture can train us to be sensitive to different fashions. So, you can't measure modesty simply by what is or is not on the body. You must also analyze what is in the heart.

Contemporary American culture, by our language, tends to limit modesty to dress. We have one word for modesty and expect it to bear the weight of

56

both the visual modesty as well as the type we can't see. Other languages, including contemporary French, use at least two words to speak of both sexual, physical modesty and that of inner modesty. The Greek culture had *four* words for modesty to differentiate between that which was external and that which was internal. Are we missing something in our culture?

Peter challenges you and me to be careful about inner modesty. He says, **"Your beauty** should not come from outward adornment, such as braided hair and the wearing of gold jewelry and fine clothes. Instead, it should be that of your inner self, **the unfading beauty of a gentle and quiet spirit, which is of great worth in God's sight."**

He's not so much dissing the fashions as he is calling women to a higher and much more challenging presentation of modesty . . . that of inner confidence.

Queen Vashti, Esther's predecessor, is the Bible's hidden hero. The king called her to flaunt herself. He and his friends were drunk, and she knew it was inappropriate for a woman in her culture to flaunt her beauty in front of a man, let alone a room full of drunken men. She lost her crown but not her honor. She oozed with inner confidence!

Queen Vashti understood that the power of her allure was protected not only by *what* she wore but also by *where* she went, *when* she went there, and *how* she

acted. She held the power of inner modesty in the palm of her hand. She wasn't about to forfeit that power . . . not even at the command of the king.

I read recently that new Christian artist Joy Williams doesn't hug a guy from the front. She only gives guys "side hugs," avoiding the weakness that her beautiful body against theirs could awaken. She's displaying inner modesty in how she approaches guys. Very cool!

[You cannot limit the power of your modesty to just what you wear]. It's also controlled or forfeited by where you are willing to go with guys, when you go there, and how you act. I bet you can think of a girl whose reputation as a flirt precedes her . Perhaps she does not dress to show off the secrets of her beauty, but the way she invades a guy's personal space or flirts with him issues an unspoken challenge concerning her sexuality.

What's so strangely twisted about immodesty is that such exhibitionism is really masked insecurity. It's like the girl who can't stop talking about herself. Have you ever been around one of those types? Within minutes you can see right past all the bragging to the insecure girl that she really is. The girl who is confident with herself finds no need to flaunt and flirt around guys.

Which brings me back to the naked statue. Remember her from the first chapter? She's simply called *The Greek Slave*. She has no name, and yet she has become a dear symbol to me of inner modesty. The sculptor, Hiram Powers, says the young woman represented by the statue was the last member of her family left to live after the Greek islands were attacked by the Turks. Her beauty and youth made her valuable to the Turks, and so she was to be kept and sold as a sex slave. As we see her, she stands fully nude with just her hand covering her most intimate parts. A cross and locket, visible among the drapery she's been required to remove, indicate she is a Christian. Her downward gaze does not say what Bathsheba's did, nor what Britney Spears's did. Instead, her inner confidence shines through and she seems to rise above her degradation with an inner purity and character. (That confidence is certainly not about what she's wearing!)

More than one hundred thousand people traveled to see her during her 1847–48 American tour. Protestant ministers applauded the work despite her sensational situation—that of a woman on sale as a sex slave—because her inward purity is evident. That is the great paradox of Hiram's work.

Greek Slave, Detail, ©The Newark Museum

[Modesty *is* a great paradox.] Though an immodest woman creates insatiable curiosity in a guy, it is the modest girl whose heart he most desires. Her modesty is first noted by her external presentation, but if it's not followed by the confidence of internal modesty, she forfeits the power of her virtue. Crazy, isn't it?

Greek Slave, Detail, ©The Newark Museum

How can I explain what internal modesty looks like? It's seen in the girl who doesn't hang all over guys but acknowledges them nonchalantly as she might another girl. Internal modesty is seen in the girl whose morning dress routine helps her reflect God's beauty but does not find her obsessing in front of the mirror. It's

Singer-songwriter **REBECCA ST. JAMES** counts on her family to keep her accountable in everything including modesty. Her sense of style, reflective of her musical variety, ranges from earth-toned prints to vivid colors. What shines through is not her body but her genuine beauty.

Who do you think is a consistently **BEAUTIFUL** example of modesty in today's contemporary Christian culture?

"REBECCA ST. JAMES. SHE'S JUST THE REAL THING. SHE'S VERY GENUINE AND VERY CAUTIOUS ABOUT WHAT SHE WEARS. SHE'S VERY, VERY INTENSE ABOUT SEEKING GOD'S WILL NOT JUST WHILE SHE'S ON STAGE BUT WHEN SHE'S OFF STAGE OR WHEN SHE'S ALONE OR WHEN SHE'S WITH A GROUP OF PEOPLE WHO DON'T EVEN KNOW WHO SHE IS. SHE IS BEAUTIFUL. IF ANYONE WOULD HAVE REASON TO FLAUNT, REBECCA WOULD. SHE'S GOT A GREAT BODY. SHE'S A GOOD-LOOKING YOUNG LADY, BUT SHE DOESN'T FLAUNT IT. SHE CONSISTENTLY DRESSES IN A MODEST FORM."

--SUSIE SHELLENBERGER, EDITOR, BRIO

seen in the girl who requires a guy to do the pursuing . . . in the girl whose conversation revolves more around other people than herself . . . in the girl who's obviously more in love with Jesus than the idea of a boyfriend.

Have you ever met a beautiful girl only to find that her stunning looks fade as her personality comes through? Ever heard about the girl whose reputation precedes her as the class flirt? Have you sat quietly watching the girl who consistently boasts and hangs on guys? Then you've seen the girl who lacks inner modesty.

Ever met a girl who becomes more and more attractive as you get to know her? Then you've seen internal modesty. This is the girl who's so confident in her value that she has no reason to immodestly flaunt herself but confidently blesses you and others when she is around.

So, which girl are you? Have you taken time to consider not only what you wear, but where you go, when you go there, and how you act when you are there?

get this! A girl's modesty is first noted by her external presentation, but if it's not followed by the confidence of inner modesty, she still forfeits the power of her virtue.

NOTE
1. 1 Peter 3:3–4.

CHAPTER 6

[The Bottom Line]

It was late 2001. One girl's life was about to change . . . all because a teen call-in show talked about modesty.

The phone lines rang that night. Girls like Sarah called in. She told a story of how she'd worn jeans that were too tight to the movies and ended up attracting a really creepy guy. She was so scared that she and her cousin ended up calling one of their dads to pick them up.

A few minutes later, Jamie called in.

"Yeah, I was listening to what Sarah said and that she didn't realize she'd worn jeans that were too tight. As a Christian, when we find ourselves in that situation where we have worn something too tight, too low, too short, and a guy starts stalking us, all we have to do is pray and God will come through for us. That's the answer," ascertained Jamie.

Radio cohost Susie Shellenberger didn't waste words telling Jamie she was wrong.

"Jamie, I have a real problem with that. It sounds like what you're saying is that you can wear what you want to and then when you get yourself into trouble, you can call on God. The problem doesn't start

there. It starts when you are in your bedroom putting on that pair of jeans and when you're pulling that shirt out of your drawer. Right there is when you need to talk to God," challenged Susie.

A hot but kind debate followed. Jamie didn't "get it." Susie wasn't about to let her off the hook.

Finally, Jamie said something with the intention of rocking Susie, but it ended up rocking her own world.

"Well," said Jamie, "we can't really know what God thinks."

"We can't?" asked Susie.

"Well, no," said Jamie. "We can't know what God thinks about this pair of jeans or this shirt."

"Yeah, we really can," responded Susie. "It's this thing called prayer where we talk to God and He will actually talk back to us. It's a conversation."

After a long pause Jamie said, "Well, I'm a Christian and I don't know what God thinks."

That's when Susie brought in the big question.

"That makes me want to ask you something," said Susie. "What is a Christian?"

WHAT? WHAT IS A CHRISTIAN?

Jamie awkwardly grasped for an answer based upon going to church. The more she talked, the more Susie realized that Jamie knew a lot about God, but she didn't have a personal relationship with Him. Within minutes, Jamie was praying to ask Jesus into her heart.

A new life was about to begin for her.

That really happened on a "Life on the Edge Live" radio broadcast. I changed the girl's name and shortened it a bit, but that powerful, amazing conversation actually took place on live radio!

I hope Jamie finds that she really can hear God's voice now . . . and obey it.

Jamie's stubborn thinking about modesty reminds me of my own, even as an adult.

[What about you?]

Do you find all this modesty stuff hard to swallow? Have I ruffled your feathers? Would you rather not know these simple truths I've taught you because it means you have to either reject or embrace them?

Let me be honest with you. If you are aggravated with this or are planning to ignore it, you probably don't have a modesty problem. You have a love problem.

You see, when you truly love God, you obey Him.
His guidelines for living may still be hard to swallow, but you still follow them because you realize it's about *loving Him*.

[John 14:21 says,] "Whoever has my commands and obeys them, he is the one who loves me. He who loves me will be loved by my Father, and I too will love him and show myself to him."

If you are struggling to obey God in the area of modesty, maybe it's because you do not love God. It's easy to know about God and His Son. Lots of people do. Most Americans do, actually. But few know Him. And when you do truly know Him, you can't help but love Him, because you realize everything in His plan for your life is for the purpose of blessing you.

Let me review where we've been so that you can see very clearly on one page what God desires for you.

 Modesty is a delicate yet formidable power that God has given to you.

 God's intended purpose for you as a carefully crafted masterpiece is to "intoxicate" one man with the fullest extent of your beauty.

 Since immodesty creates arousal in many men, it misses the mark of God's intended purpose for you. It's not just fashion. It's sin.

 The allure of immodesty is not in what is seen but what is not seen. Modesty issues a challenge for one man to romantically earn your virtue.

 A girl's modesty is first noted by her external presentation, but if it's not followed by the confidence of internal modesty, she still forfeits the power of her virtue.

And now, this:

 Modesty is possible only if you truly love God. When you love Him, you will be able to obey Him in the way that you dress.

Make no mistake. **It is God who desires for you to dress modestly and to save the secrets of your beauty for one man.** First Timothy 2:9–10 says, "I also want women to dress modestly . . . not with braided hair or gold or pearls or expensive clothes, but with good deeds, appropriate for women who profess to worship God." It's only right that a girl who claims to love Christ would reflect it in the way she dresses. First Corinthians 6:19–20 even takes it so far as to remind us that our bodies are the temple of God and we are called to honor Him with them.

Why? Why does God impose guidelines on our fashion? Deuteronomy 6:20–21, 24 says, "In the future, when your son asks you, 'What is the meaning of the . . . laws the LORD our God has commanded you?' tell him . . . 'The LORD commanded us to obey all these decrees and to fear the LORD our God, so that we might always *prosper* . . .'" (italics added). God's guidelines in this area of modesty are to enable you to live prosperously in your love life! He loves you and deeply desires to see you happy! He knows that the best pathway to finding a truly blessed marriage requires you to live modestly.

Do you love Him?

As I've struggled with how to leave you, I'm compelled to leave you with the words of One who loves you so much that He died for you. If Jesus were to write you a love note, I think this is what it would say. . . .

["My Precious Masterpiece:]

Have the bad-hair days and hormones gotten the worst of you? Oh, if only you could see how brilliant a masterpiece you are.

I couldn't wait for you to arrive. You! Yes, you! I've anticipated your presence on My earth before it was even created.

Like a master embroiderer sits at his loom painstakingly interweaving each unique strand, I knit you together piece by piece with intention and precision. You are one of the unique expressions of My own glory. I chose the color of your hair from the earth and the color of your eyes from the brilliance of My skies. I even placed My thumb there on your nose, marking it with My fingerprint.

After you were made in secret, I revealed you to this world with still the most profound parts of your beauty waiting to be crafted. Still, I am creating you in secret, My masterpiece.

Though the full secrets of your beauty are unknown to the world, I see. And I am enthralled by your beauty.

Oh, how I love you.

There have been only two places on earth that I have been willing to fill with My own radiant glory—the old temple . . . and you! That's how precious your body is to Me.

Will you honor Me with it?

Will you love Me back?

                                               Your Master Craftsman, Jesus"*

*This letter from Jesus is written using Ephesians 1:4–7; Psalm 139:13–16; Psalm 45:11–14; 1 Corinthians 6:19–20.

[Do you love Him?]

Oh, we all stray from time to time. I dare to admit that even in my own closet right now there is an outfit I can think of that needs to go! I don't want to get rid of it because I really like it, but . . . do I love Him? Yes, I do. Do you? Take some time right now to write Him a love letter. The last spread of this book is a head start for you to **write your own love letter to God** based on the six simple truths we've explored in this book. Each truth is listed once again. Your job is to rephrase it into a statement or paragraph to God that is personal for you. You'll be confessing and embracing, setting goals and erasing old mistakes as you write.

For example, for number 1, which says, "Modesty is a delicate yet formidable power that God has given to you," I would write this: "God, I'm sorry that at times I truly gave the power away, sometimes without knowing it . . . and other times because I enjoyed the sense of power it gave me. I realize this power was misused, and I am sorry. Help me to develop a formidable sense of power in this gift of modesty so that I can protect my marriage."

This love letter to God is sort of a personal creed to enable you to access the power of your modesty. I pray that in some small way it will help you to keep the most powerful secrets of your beauty for just one man. I can't make it any easier, but I hope that by God's Spirit this book has at least explained to you *why* it is so vital to be a secret keeper. It's a tough job to keep such beauty under wraps, but as the Bible says, the waiting is what makes it so sweet to share with one man in God's time!

"Your body is a temple of the Holy Spirit, who is in you, whom you have received from God . . . You are not your own; you were bought at a price. Therefore honor God with your body." --1 Corinthians 6:19–20

1

Modesty is a delicate yet formidable power that God has given to you.

2

God's intended purpose for you as a carefully crafted masterpiece is to "intoxicate" one man with the fullest extent of your beauty.

....
....
....
....
....
....
....
....
....
....
....
....
....

3 Since immodesty creates arousal in many men, it misses the mark of God's intended purpose for you. It's not just fashion. It's sin.

4

The allure of immodesty is not in what is seen but what is not seen. Modesty issues a challenge for one man to romantically earn your virtue.

....

....

....

....

....

....

....

....

....

....

....

....

....

....

....

5 A girl's modesty is first noted by her external presentation, but if it's not followed by the confidence of internal modesty, she still forfeits the power of her virtue.

....

....

....

....

....

....

....

....

....

....

....

....

Modesty is possible only if you truly love God. When you love Him, you will be able to obey Him in the way that you dress.

....

....

....

....

....

....

....

....

....

....

....

....

....